The
Cannabis Colle...
Coloring Book for Adults

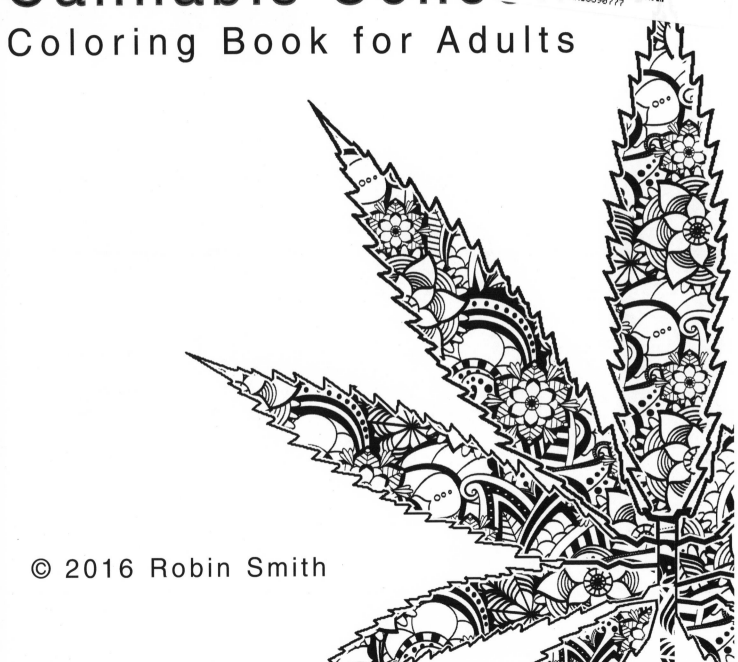

© 2016 Robin Smith

Cannabis seeds were used as a food source in China dating back to 6000 B.C.

Cannabis seeds contain all the amino acids needed by humans. A person can be sustained indefinitely from eating cannabis seeds alone and receive all her/his required amino acids.

The oldest known reference to cannabis for medical purposes dates back to 2727 B.C.

Cannabis was detected on smoking pipes found in the garden of William Shakespeare.

Prior to being banned, hemp was a staple cash crop of the family farm in early America.

In the colonial U.S., hemp was harvested and used for clothing, sails, and rope.

The first law in the American colonies covering marijuana was put in place in 1619 . This law required farmers to grow hemp.

The first two drafts of the Declaration of Independence were written on paper made from hemp.

Prior to 1942, marijuana was listed in the U.S. Pharmacopoeia as a treatment for nausea, rheumatism, and labor pains.

In 1996, California became the first state to legally allow medical marijuana.

As progressive as California may seem now, it was the first state to pass a law banning marijuana.

Recently, Colorado has gained notoriety for legalizing marijuana. However, Alaska legalized marijuana for personal use in 1975.

The first arrest ever for possessing and selling marijuana occurred in Colorado.

A compound derived from cannabis stops metastasis in aggressive cancers.

Cannabis is the largest crop in the U.S. by cash value.

The word "Canvas" is a derivative of "Cannabis". In the past, canvas was made from hemp fiber.

The cannabis plant can grow in nearly any environment and averages one to two inches of growth per day and up to 18 feet total in ideal conditions.

Supporters of medical marijuana say it has significant medical value in treatments for AIDS, glaucoma, cancer, multiple sclerosis, epilepsy, and chronic pain.

THC has been found to inhibit the growth of cancer cells in the liver.

Cannabis plants can be used to remove radioactive contaminants in the soil.

There are no recorded cases of anyone overdosing on marijuana. A lethal dose would require the consumption of 1,500 pounds within 15 minutes.

One study indicated it would require 800 joints for marijuana to become lethal, but the cause of death would be from carbon monoxide poisoning not from an overdose.

The first product sold/bought over the internet was marijuana.

In 2014, the DEA spent an average of $4.20 for every marijuana plant they uprooted (but that's not where the term 420 came from).

Four individuals in the U.S. receive legal shipments of marijuana, which is supplied to them by the U.S. government for free.

Other amazing adult coloring books available on Amazon.com:

Reefer Madness Mandala and
Quote Coloring Book for Adults

Mandalas and More
Adult Coloring Book

International Swear Words
A Foul Language Coloring Book
for Adults...

The Ultimate
Adult Coloring Book for Men

Interesting Reading

- http://antiquecannabisbook.com/chap2B/China/China.htm

- http://nowiknow.com/license-to-toke/

- http://time.com/3990305/william-shakespeare-cannabis-marijuana-high/

- http://www.huffingtonpost.com/2012/09/19/marijuana-and-cancer_n_1898208.html

- http://www.huffingtonpost.com/2013/08/11/marijuana-history-united-states_n_3736586.html

- http://www.mhhe.com/biosci/pae/botany/botany_map/articles/article_10.html

- http://www.princeton.edu/~achaney/tmve/wiki100k/docs/Marihuana_Tax_Act_of_1937.html

- http://www.theweedblog.com/how-much-marijuana-does-it-take-for-someone-to-overdose/

- https://en.wikibooks.org/wiki/Marijuana_Cultivation/Fundamentals/Parts_of_the_Plant#Seeds

- https://en.wikipedia.org/wiki/Cash_crop#United_States

- https://scholar.google.com/scholar_case?case=245698136814114591&q=%22204+P.3d+364%22&hl=en&as_sdt=2002

- https://www.ncbi.nlm.nih.gov/pubmed/21475304

- https://www.theguardian.com/science/2013/apr/19/online-high-net-drugs-deal

- https://www.washingtonpost.com/news/wonk/wp/2016/04/15/the-government-spent-18-million-destroying-marijuana-plants-last-year/

Made in the USA
San Bernardino, CA
14 November 2018